BY AJIT SINGH

COMPUTER STORYBOOK

FOR KIDS

AGE GROUP 4-6 Years

Computer Storybook For Kids
Age Group 4-6 Years

Ajit Singh
ajit_singh24@yahoo.com

Preface

Children have a never-ending curiosity about the world around them and frequently question how and why it works the way it does. The children are interested in causal information, but had not yet linked this to a real-world activity, such as reading. A new study finds that children prefer causally-rich storybooks, suggesting that such content may be more engaging and could help to increase children's interest in reading computer.

Children have an insatiable appetite to understand why things are the way they are, leading to their apt description as "little scientists. Children's interest in causal information regarding the computer, they didn't know whether it influenced children's preferences during real-world activities, such as reading. Children have an insatiable appetite to understand why things are the way they are, leading to their apt description as "little scientists.

Finding the factors that motivate children to read books is important. Encouraging children to read more improves their early literacy and language skills and could get them off to a running start with their education. Reading books in the company of a parent or teacher is a great way for children to start reading, and simply choosing the types of story book that children most prefer could be an effective way to keep them interested and motivated.

This story book is designed for the age group 4-6 years, carefully matched storybooks to the children.
The children appeared to be equally as interested and enthusiastic while reading story book. However, when asked which book they preferred they tended to choose the book loaded with causal information, suggesting that the children were influenced by storybook . "I believe this result may be due to children's natural desire to learn about how the world works,"

This book is devoted to **World Literecy Foundation, Australia.**

"Well Joha, are you ready to come to work with me today?"
"Sure Dad." "Can I take Zip?" Dad."

"Good morning Smith. Joha is visiting me at work today." "Well, hello there Joha,
"said Smith."Hope you have fun today!"

"This is where I do my work," said Dad. "This is my computer."

"This is my monitor," he continued, "I use the monitor to see what I'm doing on
the computer."

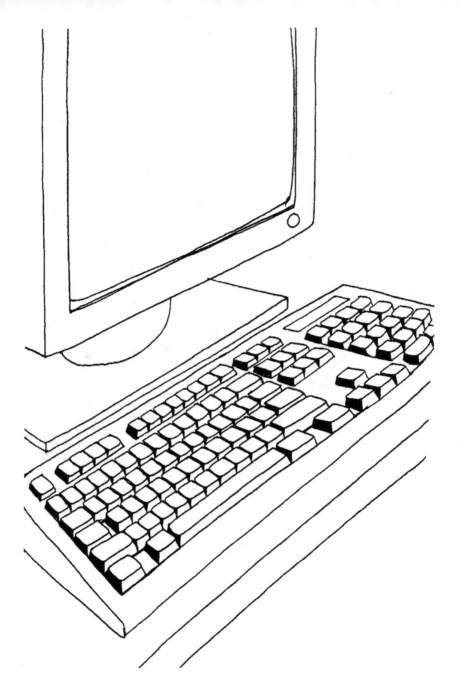

"and this is the KEYBOARD. I use the keyboard to type in words on the computer."

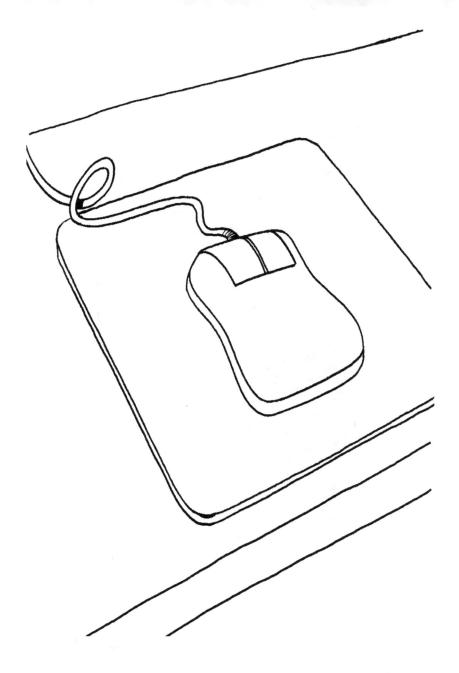

"I also use this thing to do work on my computer. It's called a MOUSE."
Joha laughed. "It doesn't look like a mouse to me!"

Dad showed her some more parts to the computer. "These are the SPEAKERS.

Any sound that the computer makescomes out of the speakers."

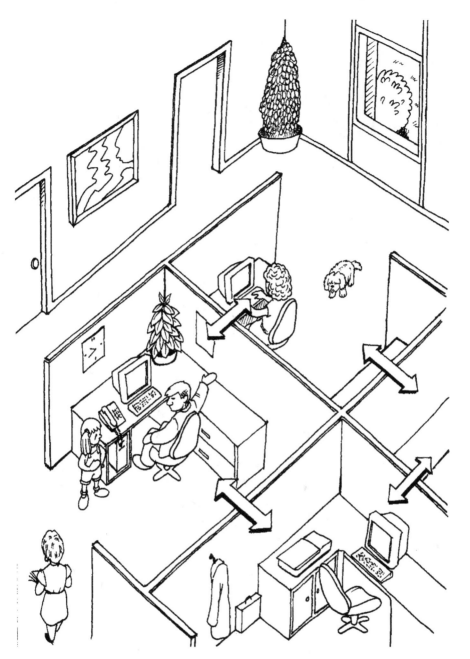

"My computer is connected to all the other computers in this room," said Joha's
Dad, "when this happens it means I'm on a NETWORK." "A network allows me
to send FILES to any of the other workers."
"What's a file?" asked Joha.

"Oops! I forgot this is all new to you Joha. A FILE is whatI want to send --
like a message."
"You mean I can send a message to that computer from your computer?"
asked Joha.
"Sure, watch this..."

Joha suddenly looked around the room. "Hey, wait a minute! Where's Zip?!"

"You look over there," said Dad, "and I'll look over here."

Help Joha, Dad and Zip get to work. Draw a line from START to FINISH.

"Here Zip!" called Joha.

"Hi, my name is Joha and I'm looking for my dog, hisname is Zip."
"Hi Joha, my name is John and I haven't seen Zip.""What does he look like?"

"Here, I have a picture of Zip."

"I've got an idea," John said, "let's SCAN the picture into the computer and make a poster to hang up." "Great!" Joha replied. "Where do we start?"

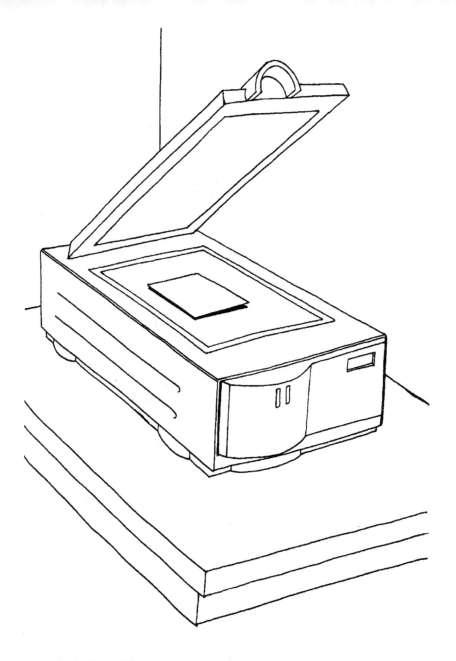

"This is our **SCANNER.**" "First we place the picture facedown on the **FLATBED SCANNER.**" "Then we move our mouse, which makes the pointer on the screen move."

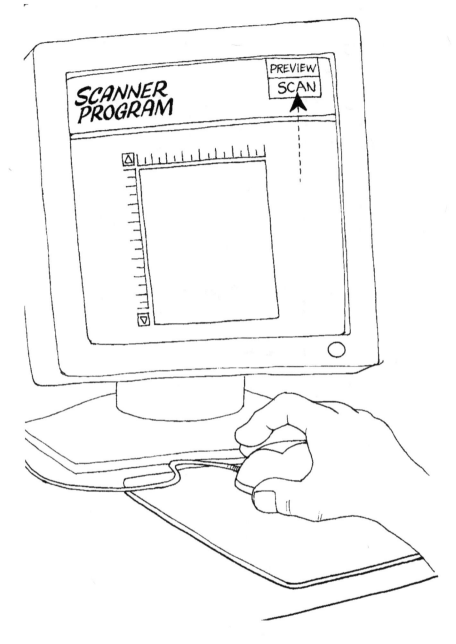

"We move the pointer over the button that says SCAN." "If we quickly press and release the left mouse button twice the scanner starts scanning."

"There you are," said John. "The scanner put a picture of Zip on the screen. This is called a GRAPHIC. Now, using the keyboard we can type in the word missing.

"After making the sign we can print it out by clicking the PRINT button."

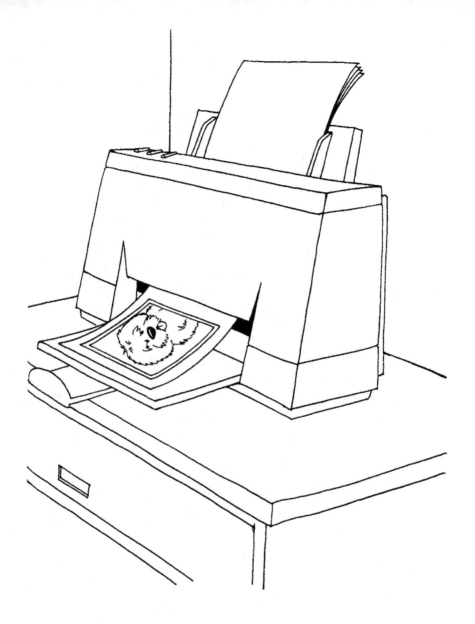

"See Joha, the printer makes the actual paper copy of what you see on the computer screen.""Thank you John", said Joha.
"I'm glad I could help", said John. "I'll print some more copies for you to hangup."